D1347843

Cooking
with kids

K

A Pyramid Cookery Paperback

Cooking
with kids

hamlyn

An Hachette Livre UK Company
www.hachettelivre.co.uk

A Pyramid Paperback

First published in Great Britain in 2008 by
Hamlyn, a division of Octopus Publishing Group Ltd
2–4 Heron Quays, London E14 4JP
www.octopusbooks.co.uk

ISBN 978-0-600-61809-6

A CIP catalogue record for this book is available from the British Library

Printed and bound in China

10 9 8 7 6 5 4 3 2 1

Notes
Both metric and imperial measurements have been given in all recipes. Use one set of measurements only, and not a mixture of both.

Standard level spoon measurements are used in all recipes.
1 tablespoon = one 15 ml spoon
1 teaspoon = one 5 ml spoon

All eggs used in the recipes are medium.

Ovens should be preheated to the specified temperature – if using a fan-assisted oven, follow the manufacturer's instructions for adjusting the time and the temperature.

This book includes dishes made with nuts and nut derivatives. It is advisable for those with known allergic reactions to nuts and nut derivatives and those who may be potentially vulnerable to these allergies, such as pregnant and nursing mothers, invalids, the elderly, babies and small children, to avoid foods made with nuts. It is also prudent to check the labels of pre-prepared ingredients for the possible inclusion of nut derivatives.

Children should be supervised by an adult at all times when cooking or baking. The tasks that can be performed at a particular age or stage in their development will differ from child to child.

Contents

Introduction

It is a joy to cook with children of all ages, even if it can get rather messy. Children's energy and enthusiasm for cooking are an inspiration, and any doubts that some of the trickier tasks like kneading or piping are beyond their young years are often quickly dispelled. Children want to be helpful, contribute to family life and copy what they see you doing. Cooking is one way that they can produce real results, ones that everyone can enjoy.

With ready meals now taking up more and more supermarket space, we are in danger of bringing up a generation of children who can't or don't want to cook. Encouraging your children to cook for themselves can only be a good thing, and this book shows how to make delicious dishes from scratch as well as teaching useful cooking techniques. Children develop at different rates but even the smallest child should be able to use a biscuit cutter, while over-sixes will be able to measure out ingredients, beat with a whisk and even knead dough.

Allow lots of time when cooking with little children – kids hate being hurried – and don't worry too much about the look of the finished product. It's the time that you've spent creating something together that's important.

First cooking experiences need to be fun so this book is full of child-friendly ideas for food that you and your little ones can easily and quickly cook together, from gooey cakes and irresistible cookies to edible Christmas decorations, tasty lunches and yummy party treats.

Boost confidence

Because cooking is an activity that uses all the senses, it totally absorbs children. It gives them a sense of achievement and confidence as they try new things. As they become older and more capable, children will be able to make their favourite foods on their own, and will develop a familiarity with food that will give them the confidence to be more creative in the kitchen in later life.

Learn to experiment

Children find it rewarding to serve up dishes they've cooked themselves, so cooking with little ones can be a great way to motivate fussy eaters. Cooking together is relaxing and, as children smell and feel the food they prepare, they may feel more confident and adventurous and more willing to try something new.

Cooking is educational

Children learn a huge amount from cooking without even realizing it. Very young children quickly learn new skills in an entertaining way – weighing and measuring introduce them to the concepts of numbers, weights, volume and accuracy, while mixing, spreading and spooning aid co-ordination. Taking children shopping for ingredients is a learning experience, too. It helps spark children's interest in food and may even encourage fussy eaters to try unfamiliar produce once back home.

Healthy eating

Cooking at home gives you control over what your children eat and by cooking from scratch you know exactly what they

are consuming. Kids can still enjoy sweet treats but without the additives most of us know little about and fear may harm their growing bodies. Instead of giving your children shop-bought produce, open their minds to the wonderful variety of textures, smells and tastes of healthier home cooking. Show them where their food comes from and how much fun it is to combine different ingredients to make yummy meals and snacks.

With just a little encouragement, a lifelong interest in real food and cooking may easily be sparked in your children at a tender age.

Cooking with kids

Here are a few basic rules to help ensure that cooking with your child is fun and goes well from beginning to end.

Be prepared

First choose your recipe, bearing in mind the ability of your child. Remember that cooking with a little one takes much longer than cooking on your own, so make sure you have plenty of time to complete the recipe. Each recipe gives an indication of the preparation time, but this will vary according to your child's age.

Next, collect together all the necessary ingredients and equipment before you start and lay them out on the work surface so you can check you've got everything you need. Most of the recipes included here use basic equipment, but check you've got any necessary tins or cutters before you start. Nothing will make you feel more fed up than getting halfway through a recipe to find that you are missing a vital ingredient or cake tin. It will also cause intense disappointment on the part of your assistant chef!

Kitchen safety

Small children must **always** be supervised in the kitchen, and kitchen equipment should be used sensibly so that accidents won't happen. Make sure you teach children about the potential dangers posed by hot ovens, full saucepans, electrical equipment and sharp knives and adhere to the following basic rules when working in the kitchen:

- Always wear oven gloves when putting things in or taking them out of the oven.
- Take special care when opening oven doors in front of children.
- Handle knives and electrical equipment with care and respect. Use a chopping board when working with a kitchen knife and never chop directly on the work surface.

Hygiene

Teach your child basic hygiene rules from an early age:

- Always wash your hands before starting to cook.
- Make sure that all your work surfaces are clean.
- Tie back long hair and remove any loose clothing or jewellery.
- Wear an apron or coverall to keep clothes clean.
- Clear up any spillages on the floor as soon as they happen.
- Use different chopping boards for raw meat and vegetables/fruit.

- Hot food can burn so stir large pans carefully and keep your hands away from steaming kettles or boiling water.
- Choose a pan that is big enough so the contents do not bubble over.
- Make sure saucepan and frying pan handles are turned to the side so they can't get knocked.
- Although most dishes do not get hot in a microwave, unglazed pottery does, and food definitely does, so handle with care.
- Only turn the hob on when you need it and never touch it as it will stay hot after you have finished cooking on it.
- Use the back rings of the hob when working with small children so they aren't tempted to grab saucepan handles from below to see what's cooking.

- Remember to turn off the oven when you have finished.
- Never place sharp knives or food processor blades in the sink, where they can easily be hidden by soap bubbles. Instead, rinse them as you go and then put them out of harm's way.

Clearing up

It is good practice to involve little ones in clearing up after cooking. Even tiny children can have a go at washing up if you give them time and encouragement.

After cooking, get your children to help you to make sure all unused ingredients are put away, all equipment is washed up and dried, all work surfaces are wiped clean and the floor is swept or mopped.

What you will need

Here is a list of some basic kitchen equipment you'll need for the recipes in this book, most of which you are likely to have at home already.

- Kitchen scales
- Measuring jug
- Chopping board
- Kitchen scissors
- Timer or clock
- Kitchen knives
- Oven gloves

- Tablespoon
- Teaspoon
- Dessertspoon
- Fork
- Mixing bowls
- Wooden spoon
- Saucepans

Child-friendly equipment

You don't have to buy any special equipment in order to cook with children, but certain items will make life easier for them so may mean they (and you) enjoy the cooking experience more.

Step-up stool It's worth investing in a child's step-up stool or a sturdy child-sized chair so that your child can see above the work surface or sink when he is cooking. Alternatively, find a low table that he can work on or cover the floor with a plastic sheet or tablecloth and then have him sit on the sheet while cooking.

Apron A little apron is a treat for small cooks. A wipe-clean one will make it particularly easy to avoid splashes and keep your little one clean. A cheaper alternative is to use an old shirt.

Digital weighing scales Digital scales are the best type of scales for children to use as the figures are clear to read, and it's easier for children to match them exactly to what's given in the recipe. Traditional balance scales can be tricky for children to use, unless they have a pointer to show that the correct weight has been reached.

Weighing and measuring

The recipes in this book are written in both metric (grams, millilitres and litres) and imperial (pounds, ounces and pints) measurements. Whichever one you choose to follow, stick with it all through the recipe; don't mix and match or the recipe may not work. Also make sure that all ingredients are carefully and accurately measured and weighed out, or again the recipe may not work.

Always use proper kitchen measuring spoons rather than ordinary teaspoons, dessertspoons, etc. This ensures that you use the exact amount needed in a recipe. For most ingredients, especially dry ones like spices, flour and baking powder, this should be a level spoonful rather than a heaped one, so level it off by gently shaking the spoon or sliding a knife across the top – a rounded measure could almost double the amount of ingredient required!

When using a measuring jug, fill it to the required level then double-check the quantity by setting the jug on a hard surface so that the contents are level.

Small wooden spoon A child-sized wooden spoon makes beating and mixing much easier for very little ones.

A set of measuring spoons These are useful for accurately measuring ingredients in whole and fractions of teaspoons and tablespoons. Everyday cutlery should not be used for measuring as the designs, depths, capacity and shapes of the spoons vary so much.

Plastic measuring jug and bowls Plastic equipment is obviously better than glass for children's use, in case of clumsy hands. You can buy these in a wide range of eye-catching colours that will appeal to kids.

Using electrical equipment

Although you can make all the recipes in this book without using the following electrical items, they will save you time and effort if used properly.

Using a microwave Always use china, plastic or heavy glass bowls (such as Pyrex) in the microwave and never use metal containers or dishes with silver or gold decoration. Unglazed pottery tends to get hot, so avoid this as well. If you need to cover food, then use microwaveable clingfilm or a plate.

Using an electric mixer Ideal for mixing cakes, whisking egg whites or making pastry. Always check that the electricity is switched off before you fix the two metal beaters in place, then switch on the whisk. Don't stir ingredients while the blades are running and turn off the electricity before you take the blades out to wash them.

Using a food processor You can use a food processor for mixing cakes, making pastry and breadcrumbs, finely chopping vegetables, blending soups or fruit until smooth and making milk shakes and fruit smoothies.

Make sure that the blade is firmly secured in the base of the processor and click the lid securely into position. As the processor motor is very powerful, blend the ingredients for just a minute or two and then have a look. If you need to add any food during blending, add it through the feeder tube at the top and keep the spoon or your fingers well above the top of the tube. Don't attempt to get anything out of the bowl until the blade has stopped turning. Remember that the blade is very sharp, so lift it from the plastic centre and not the metal edges.

Cook's terms

Introduce young children to cookery terminology as soon as they start to learn to cook, and tell them why the techniques work.

Baking To cook food in the oven.

Beating To soften an ingredient or mix it with another ingredient, usually using a wooden spoon or electric mixer.

Blending To mix foods until they become smooth.

Creaming To beat butter/margarine and sugar with a wooden spoon or an electric whisk until it forms a smooth, pale, cream-like mixture; this technique is usually used when making cakes.

Dicing To cut food into small cubes.

Draining To pour off the liquid from food through a strainer or colander.

Folding in To mix ingredients together with a very gentle stirring action to keep the air in the mixture. Use a metal spoon and gently stir the spoon through the two different mixtures in a swirling movement.

Greasing To coat a cooking utensil, such as a baking sheet or cake tin, with a little oil or butter to prevent cakes or biscuits from sticking when cooked.

Kneading To smooth the outside of dough. Grab the side of the dough nearest you and, keeping hold of it, stretch the other side of the dough down and away from you with the palm or heel of your hand. Then lift the far edge up and over into the centre. Now give the dough a quarter turn and knead again as before. Turning the dough regularly, continue for at least 10 minutes or until the dough becomes smooth, elastic and no longer sticky.

Lining To put greaseproof or nonstick baking paper into the base or the base and sides of a cake tin so the cake does not stick when cooked. The paper must be greased as well as the tin.

Sieving/Sifting To remove the lumps from dry ingredients by pressing them or shaking them through a sieve.

Simmering To cook liquid in a saucepan over a gentle heat so that bubbles just break the surface.

Whipping/Whisking To beat air into ingredients such as egg whites or cream using a hand or electric whisk so that they become very thick.

Tiny cooks

Chocolate teddies

Makes 12
Preparation time 20 minutes
Cooking time 10–15 minutes

100 g (3½ oz) butter, at
  room temperature
100 g (3½ oz) caster sugar
few drops vanilla extract
2 eggs
100 g (3½ oz) self-raising
  flour
50 g (2 oz) milk chocolate
  drops
50 g (2 oz) white chocolate
  drops

For the chocolate butter icing
150 g (5 oz) icing sugar
2 tablespoons cocoa
  powder
50 g (2 oz) butter, at room
  temperature
white and milk chocolate
  buttons/drops, to
  decorate

This easy-to-make bun mixture is studded with dark and white chocolate chips. Here the cakes are decorated as teddy bears, but let your child use her imagination.

1   Line a 12-cup patty tin with paper cases.

2   Put the butter, sugar and vanilla extract in a mixing bowl and, using a wooden spoon, beat them together until creamy.

3   Add the eggs and beat the mixture again, then sift in the flour and stir it in. Finally, stir in the chocolate drops. Spoon the mixture into the paper cases with a dessertspoon so that they are three-quarters full.

4   Place the cakes in a preheated oven, 180°C (350°F), Gas Mark 4, and bake for 10–15 minutes or until risen and golden. Remove them from the oven and allow to cool for a few minutes then transfer them to a wire rack and leave to cool completely.

5   Meanwhile, make the chocolate butter icing by sifting the icing sugar and cocoa into a bowl, adding the butter, then beating the ingredients together until the mixture is smooth.

6   When the cakes are cool, spread them with the icing. Use a fork to make the icing look like fur and then decorate them, making eyes, ears and a nose.

Butterfly biscuits

Makes 20

Preparation time 30
minutes, plus chilling

Cooking time 10–15 minutes

275 g (9 oz) self-raising
flour, plus extra for
dusting

1 dessertspoon cinnamon
(optional)

100 g (3½ oz) soft light
brown sugar

75 g (3 oz) butter, cut into
pieces

1 egg

2 tablespoons golden syrup

For the butter icing

50 g (2 oz) butter, at room
temperature

150 g (5 oz) icing sugar

2 teaspoons milk

few drops food colouring
(optional)

To decorate

cake decorations or small
sweets

icing pens

The perfect thing to bake on a wet day. Not only will children love cutting out the butterfly shapes, but they will spend ages creatively decorating the biscuits.

1   Sift the flour and cinnamon, if using, into a bowl. Stir in the sugar.

2   Add the butter pieces and rub the mixture together with your fingertips until it resembles breadcrumbs.

3   Crack the egg and carefully break it into a measuring jug. Add the syrup and beat it with a fork. Add to the flour mix and stir into a ball. Place the dough in a plastic bag and chill for 1 hour.

4   Line 2 large baking sheets with nonstick baking paper.

5   Sprinkle some flour on the work surface and place the chilled dough in the middle. Roll or press out the dough to a thickness of 5 mm (¼ inch). Using a butterfly-shaped cutter, cut out about 20 biscuits and place on the lined baking sheets.

6   Place the biscuits in a preheated oven, 160°C (325°F), Gas Mark 3, and bake them for 10–15 minutes or until golden brown around the edges, then remove from the oven. Allow to cool on the baking sheets for a few minutes, then transfer to a wire rack to cool completely.

7   Meanwhile, make the butter icing by mixing the ingredients together in a small bowl with a wooden spoon or electric mixer.

8   Use a teaspoon to dollop and/or spread the icing over the cool biscuits. Decorate by pressing in small sweets and/or cake decorations and drawing with the icing pens.

Iced blueberry and white chocolate muffins

Makes 12
Preparation time 20 minutes
Cooking time 15 minutes

If your children enjoy blueberries as much as grown-ups do, then they will love these muffins. Don't worry if you don't get a chance to ice them, they will still taste great.

150 g (5 oz) caster sugar
50 g (2 oz) butter or
  margarine, at room
  temperature
1 egg
150 g (5 oz) self-raising flour
100 ml (3½ fl oz) milk
1 teaspoon vanilla extract
100 g (3½ oz) fresh
  blueberries
50 g (2 oz) white chocolate
  drops

For the icing
25 g (1 oz) fresh blueberries,
  plus extra for decorating
125 g (4 oz) icing sugar

1 Line a 12-cup muffin tin with paper cases.

2 Place the sugar and butter in a large mixing bowl and mash them together vigorously with a wooden spoon. Add the egg to the mixture.

3 Sift in the flour and stir it briefly. Finally, add the milk, vanilla extract, blueberries and white chocolate drops and quickly stir them in too. Using a dessertspoon, fill each paper case two-thirds full.

4 Place the muffins in a preheated oven, 190°C (375°F), Gas Mark 5, and cook them for 15 minutes, then allow the cooked muffins to cool in the tin.

5 Make the icing by placing a handful of the fresh blueberries in a small saucepan with 4 tablespoons of water and heat gently on the hob. Mash the blueberries with the back of a wooden spoon until you have a bright purple mush, then remove from the heat and strain through a sieve or strainer into a small mixing bowl.

6 Sift in the icing sugar and stir together to make a smooth, purple glacé icing.

7 Place the muffins on a large serving plate and drizzle the icing on to the top of them with a teaspoon. Decorate the iced muffins by pressing a blueberry on to the top of each one.

Mini quiches

Makes 18
Preparation time 45 minutes
Cooking time 20 minutes

These little quiches are fun to make and can be filled with your child's favourite foods. They are great for lunchboxes and picnics too.

a little cooking oil, for
   greasing
plain flour, for dusting
375 g (12 oz) ready-rolled
   shortcrust pastry, thawed
   if frozen and taken out
   of the refrigerator
   15 minutes before use
2 eggs
200 ml (7 fl oz) milk
pinch of salt
4 slices ham, diced
2 spring onions, chopped
5 cherry tomatoes, chopped
50 g (2 oz) Cheddar cheese,
   grated

1 Sprinkle some oil into the cups of two 12-cup patty tins. Smear the oil all over the cups.

2 Sprinkle some flour on to a work surface and unroll the pastry. Flatten it with the balls of your hands. Stamp circles out of the pastry using an 8 cm (3½ inch) plain or fluted cutter and place each circle in a cup of the tin, gently pressing it down with your fingertips.

3 Place the eggs, milk and salt in a measuring jug and beat with a fork.

4 Put the ham, spring onions and cherry tomatoes into a bowl and mix together. Put a dessertspoonful of the mixture into each pastry cup.

5 Pour some of the egg and milk mixture into each cup. Sprinkle some grated cheese over the top.

6 Place the tins in a preheated oven, 220°C (425°F), Gas Mark 7, and bake the quiches for 20 minutes or until set and golden. Eat them hot or cold.

Cheesy twists

Makes about 15
Preparation time 15 minutes
Cooking time 8–12 minutes

Your child is bound to love getting messy when rubbing the cheesy mixture together in his hands, so you might want to invest in an apron!

50 g (2 oz) Cheddar cheese
75 g (3 oz) self-raising flour,
    plus extra for dusting
½ teaspoon mustard
    powder
50 g (2 oz) butter, cold and
    cut into small pieces
1 egg yolk

1 Line 2 baking sheets with nonstick baking paper.

2 Grate the cheese into a large mixing bowl, then sift the flour and mustard powder into the bowl.

3 Add the butter to the mix and rub the cheese, butter and flour together between your thumbs and fingers until the butter is broken up and covered in flour and the mixture looks like fine breadcrumbs.

4 Add the egg yolk to the mixture. Stir with a wooden spoon until you have a stiff dough.

5 Sprinkle lots of flour over a work surface and put the dough in the middle. Shape the dough with your hands and roll it with a floured rolling pin until it is about 5 mm (¼ inch) thick.

6 Take a sharp knife and cut the dough into long strips, about 1 cm (½ inch) thick. Carefully pick up each strip and twist it gently before laying it on one of the prepared baking sheets.

7 Place the twists in a preheated oven, 220°C (425°F), Gas Mark 7, and bake for 8–12 minutes until golden brown, then remove them from the oven and allow to cool on the baking sheets.

Bread monsters

Makes 8
Preparation time 30 minutes, plus rising
Cooking time 15–20 minutes

a little cooking oil, for greasing
350 g (11½ oz) strong white flour, plus extra for dusting
1 teaspoon salt
3 g (½ sachet) fast-action dried yeast
1 tablespoon vegetable oil
200 ml (7 fl oz) preboiled warm water
a few currants, to decorate
1 egg, beaten, to glaze

Making bread is easy and great fun. For tiny toddlers, you can make up the dough and then let them play with it to their heart's content.

1 Sprinkle a few drops of cooking oil on a large baking sheet and smear it over with your fingers.

2 Sift the flour and salt in a large mixing bowl and add the yeast, vegetable oil and water. Mix everything together with the wooden spoon, then put your hands into the bowl and draw the mixture together into a firm dough. If the mixture is too dry to come together, add a little more water. If the mixture is too sticky and sticks to your hands, add some more flour.

3 Sprinkle flour over the work surface and tip the dough on to it. Knead the dough by pushing, folding and turning it. You can be brutal with it: the more work, the better. Knead it for at least 5 minutes.

4 Break the dough into 8 pieces and knead into balls. Make a pointy snout at one end of each ball and place on the baking sheet. Leave plenty of space between the rolls as they will double in size. Make the prickles by snipping into the dough with the tips of scissors. Press in halved currants for eyes and whole ones for noses.

5 Cover the rolls with a clean tea towel. Leave in a warm place for 1 hour or until they have doubled in size.

6 Brush the rolls with the beaten egg and place in a preheated oven, 230°C (450°F), Gas Mark 8. Bake for 15–20 minutes. If the rolls are cooked they will sound hollow when tapped on the bottom (remember to pick them up with oven gloves as they will be hot). Transfer to a wire rack to cool.

Courgette and cheese muffins

Makes 12
Preparation time 15 minutes
Cooking time 20–25 minutes

These delicious savoury muffins are very quick to make. Apart from grating the cheese and the courgettes, they are simple enough for children to put together all by themselves.

175 g (6 oz) courgettes, grated
200 g (7 oz) Cheddar cheese, grated
250 g (8 oz) self-raising flour
1 teaspoon bicarbonate of soda
½ teaspoon salt
200 ml (7 fl oz) milk
1 egg
4 tablespoons olive oil

1   Line a 12-cup muffin tin with paper cases.

2   Place the courgettes and cheese in a mixing bowl, sift in the flour, bicarbonate of soda and salt and mix together.

3   Put the milk, egg and olive oil in a measuring jug and mix together with a fork. Pour this mixture into the other ingredients and stir until just mixed. Use a dessertspoon to spoon the mixture into the muffin cases so that each is nearly full.

4   Put the muffins in a preheated oven, 190°C (375°F), Gas Mark 5, and bake for 20–25 minutes or until risen, golden and firm to the touch. Leave them to cool in the tin for at least 10 minutes, then transfer to a wire rack. Eat hot or cold.

Pink blush strawberry smoothie

Makes 1 large glass or
  2 smaller ones
Preparation time 10 minutes

Smoothies are packed full of goodness. Why not encourage your child to try different flavour combinations such as mango and lime or raspberry and blueberry?

4 strawberries
1 small ripe banana
1 ripe peach or nectarine
150 g (5 oz) pot strawberry
  yogurt
1 teaspoon honey
150 ml (¼ pint) apple or
  orange juice

1 Remove the green tops of the strawberries, then cut the strawberries into pieces. Peel and thickly slice the banana. Cut the peach or nectarine in half, take out the stone and slice thickly.

2 Put all the fruits into a food processor or liquidizer. Add the yogurt, honey and fruit juice.

3 Put the lid carefully on the machine and blend together. Pour into glasses and serve.

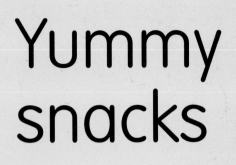

Yummy snacks

Sugared fruit pancakes

Makes 20–24
Preparation time 15 minutes
Cooking time 10 minutes

2 eggs
25 g (1 oz) unsalted butter
100 ml (3½ fl oz) milk
100 g (3½ oz) plain flour
1 teaspoon baking powder
2 tablespoons vanilla or
    caster sugar
125 g (4 oz) fresh
    blueberries
a little oil, for frying
200 g (7 oz) Greek yogurt
    (optional)

These pancakes are bursting with fresh blueberries, which release lovely sweet juices during cooking.

1   To separate the eggs, gently tap an egg on the side of a thoroughly clean bowl. Holding the egg upright, carefully ease the shells apart with your thumbs so the white falls into the bowl and the yolk is trapped in one shell half. Tip the yolk from one half of the shell to the other until most of the white has fallen into the bowl. Put the yolk in a small bowl. Separate the other egg in the same way into the two bowls.

2   Melt the butter by putting it in a small saucepan over a gentle heat. Add the milk and pour the mixture over the egg yolks, stirring well.

3   Put the flour, baking powder and 1 tablespoon of the sugar in a large bowl. Add the milk mixture and whisk well to make a smooth batter. Stir in the blueberries.

4   Whisk the egg whites until they form firm peaks when the whisk is lifted from the bowl. Spoon the whites over the batter. Using a large metal spoon, gently stir the whites into the batter until well mixed.

5   Pour a little oil into a large frying pan and heat it for 1 minute. Add a dessertspoonful of the batter to one side of the pan so it spreads to make a little cake. Add two or three more spoonfuls, so the pancakes can cook without touching. When the pancakes are golden on the underside, flip them over and cook again until golden. Using a fish slice, remove the pancakes from the pan and transfer to a serving plate, then keep them warm while you cook the remainder.

6   Sprinkle all the pancakes with the remaining sugar and serve topped with spoonfuls of yogurt, if liked.

Sausage pizza squares

Makes 6
Preparation time 25 minutes, plus rising
Cooking time 10–12 minutes

a little cooking oil, for greasing
400 g (13 oz) strong white flour, plus extra for dusting
¼ teaspoon salt
1 teaspoon caster sugar
1½ teaspoons fast-action dried yeast
2 tablespoons olive oil
200–250 ml (7–8 fl oz) warm water

For the pizza topping
4 tablespoons tomato sauce (ketchup)
3 fresh tomatoes
small bunch of fresh basil
4 cooked sausages
4 chilled frankfurters
75 g (3 oz) Cheddar cheese

Pizzas are always fun to create, and with so many different and varied toppings to choose from, you can let your child's imagination run riot!

1 Lightly brush 2 large baking sheets with a little oil.

2 Put the flour, salt, sugar and yeast into a large mixing bowl. Add the oil, then gradually mix in just enough of the warm water to mix to a soft but not sticky dough, using a wooden spoon at first, then later squeezing together with your hands.

3 Sprinkle the work surface with a little flour, then knead the dough for 5 minutes until it is smooth and elastic. Roll the dough out very thinly to a roughly shaped rectangle, about 37.5 x 25 cm (15 x 10 inches), then cut into 6 smaller equal-sized squares. Transfer the squares to the baking sheets, leaving a little space in between to allow the dough to rise and spread.

4 Spread the top of the pizzas with the tomato sauce, leaving a border of dough still showing. Cut the tomatoes into small pieces and arrange them on top of the tomato sauce, then tear the basil into pieces and sprinkle on the top. Thinly slice the cooked sausages and thickly slice the frankfurters. Arrange on top of the tomatoes, then grate the cheese and sprinkle on top. Leave the pizzas in a warm place, uncovered, to rise for 30 minutes.

5 Place the pizzas in a preheated oven, 220°C (425°F), Gas Mark 7, and bake for 10–12 minutes until the cheese is bubbling. Serve the pizzas warm with cucumber and carrot sticks – they are best eaten on the day they are made.

Tuna melts

Serves 2

Preparation time 10 minutes

Cooking time 11–13 minutes

The perfect way to introduce more fish into your child's diet, these nutritious paninis packed with tuna and sweetcorn make a quick and delicious lunch.

2 panini breads

200 g (7 oz) tuna in oil or brine

75 g (3 oz) frozen sweetcorn

3 tablespoons mayonnaise

75 g (3 oz) Gruyère or Emmenthal cheese

1 Using a bread knife, slice each panini bread in half horizontally. Tip the tuna into a sieve to drain the oil or brine. Transfer the tuna to a bowl.

2 Put the sweetcorn in a small saucepan. Boil the kettle and pour the boiled water over the sweetcorn to just cover it. Cook for 3 minutes and drain through the sieve. Rinse the sweetcorn under cold water and add it to the tuna in the bowl. Stir in the mayonnaise until well mixed.

3 Spread the tuna mixture over the two bread bases. Thinly slice the cheese and arrange on top of the tuna. Press the bread tops down firmly on the filling.

4 Heat a heavy-based frying pan or ridged grill pan for 2 minutes. Add the breads and cook on a gentle heat for 3–4 minutes on each side, turning them carefully with a fish slice or tongs. Using the fish slice, transfer the tuna melts to serving plates and serve.

Croque monsieur

Serves 2
Preparation time 15 minutes
Cooking time about
5 minutes

75 g (3 oz) Gruyère or
Cheddar cheese
15 g (½ oz) butter
1 tablespoon plain flour
125 ml (4 fl oz) milk
2 thick slices of bread
2 thick slices of ham

This extremely moreish version of cheese on toast is always a winner, so why not bring a taste of France into your kitchen? Bon appetit!

1 Coarsely grate the cheese on to a chopping board. You might need to cut off the rind if you are using Gruyère.

2 Melt the butter in a small saucepan. Sprinkle in the flour and stir it into the butter to make a paste. Cook gently, stirring, for 1 minute.

3 Remove the pan from the heat and gradually stir in the milk, stirring well until the mixture is smooth. Return the pan to the heat and stir until the sauce is thickened and bubbling. Stir in the cheese until melted.

4 Line a grill rack with a piece of foil. Put the bread on the foil and cook under a preheated moderate grill until lightly toasted on both sides. Spread each slice with 2 tablespoonfuls of the cheese sauce and lay a slice of ham on top of each. Spoon the remaining sauce over the top and spread it to the edges.

5 Grill the bread for about 3 minutes or until the topping is bubbling and beginning to brown. Use a fish slice to transfer the bread to serving plates and serve.

Popcorn

Serves 4
Preparation time 5 minutes
Cooking time 5 minutes

This is fabulous snack food for a family party or a night in with a movie. If you haven't got any maple syrup, try tossing the popcorn in jam or honey instead.

2 tablespoons sunflower oil
100 g (3½ oz) popping corn
50 g (2 oz) butter
6 tablespoons maple syrup

1   Put the oil in a large heavy-based saucepan, add the popcorn in a single layer and put the lid on the saucepan. Begin to cook over a medium heat. As the popcorn warms up you will hear loud bangs and pops as it hits the side of the pan.

2   Shake the pan from time to time to encourage the last few popcorn kernels to cook. When the pan is quiet, turn off the heat, lift the lid and carefully look inside the pan. It should be full of white puffy popcorn. If there are still lots of popcorn kernels, put the lid back on and cook for a little longer.

3   Add the butter and maple syrup to the popcorn pan and toss them together using a wooden spoon. Spoon the popcorn into coloured paper cups or cones of paper to serve.

Cashew dip with veggie dunkers

Serves 4
Preparation time 10 minutes
Cooking time 3 minutes

A delicious dip in which to dunk breadsticks, pitta bread and a colourful array of crunchy vegetables. Just remember that nuts should not be given to young children.

100 g (3½ oz) cashew nuts
200 ml (7 fl oz) Greek or
  thick natural yogurt
1 spring onion
2 teaspoons olive oil
a little paprika
2 carrots
¼ cucumber
salt and pepper

1   Line a grill pan with foil. Put the nuts on the foil and cook under a preheated moderate grill until lightly browned. When cool, tip them into a food processor or spice mill, reserving a few to garnish, and grind to make a fine powder. Mix the nuts into the yogurt.

2   Trim each end of the spring onion, then thinly slice. Stir into the nut mixture and add salt and pepper to taste. Spoon the dip into a small bowl, set on a large plate. Drizzle the dip with the olive oil and sprinkle with paprika and the reserved nuts.

3   Peel the carrots, then cut into sticks. Wash the cucumber and cut it into sticks. Arrange the veggie sticks around the dip and serve.

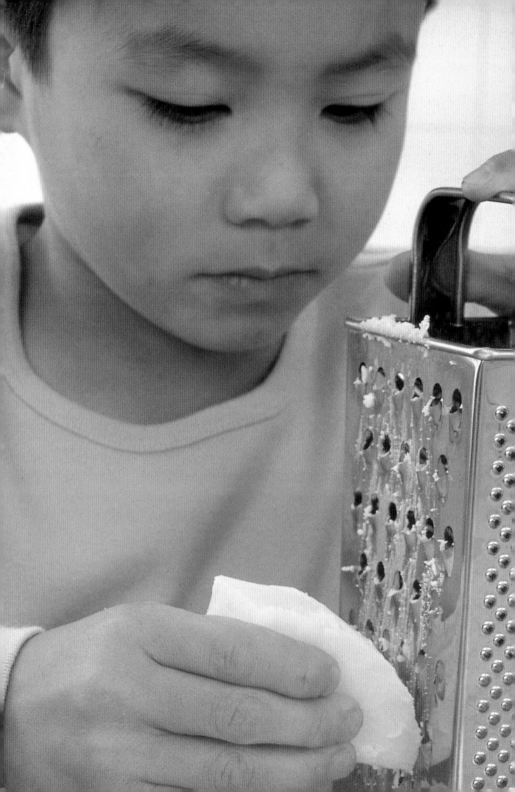

Delicious
dinners

Monster munch salad

Serves 3
Preparation time 15 minutes
Cooking time 8 minutes

Bursting with goodness, this refreshing salad is great for hungry little ones and parents alike. If you don't want to use tuna, substitute chicken or ham instead.

3 eggs
½ lemon
a few stems of fresh
  tarragon (optional)
3 tablespoons mayonnaise
1 teaspoon honey or maple
  syrup
1 cos lettuce
1 carrot
¼ cucumber
200 g (7 oz) can tuna or
  salmon in water or oil
200 g (7 oz) can cannellini
  or red kidney beans
salt and pepper

1   Put the eggs into a small saucepan, cover with cold water and bring to the boil. Simmer for 8 minutes until hard boiled.

2   Meanwhile, squeeze the lemon and snip the tarragon, if using, with scissors. Mix the lemon juice, 1 tablespoon tarragon, the mayonnaise and honey or syrup in a small bowl with a little salt and pepper.

3   Separate the lettuce leaves, throwing away the coarse outer leaves. Wash with cold water and drain in a colander. Tear into pieces and put into a large salad bowl. Drizzle the dressing over and toss together.

4   Peel the carrot, then grate into the dish. Dice the cucumber. Open the can of tuna or salmon, drain and break the fish into pieces with a fork. Open and drain the beans. Add all these ingredients to the salad bowl and mix gently.

5   Drain the hard-boiled eggs, rinse with cold water to cool quickly, crack the shells and peel the eggs. Cut the eggs into thick slices and arrange on top of the salad.

Tuna fish cakes

Makes 4
Preparation time 10 minutes
Cooking time 6 minutes

400 g (13 oz) can tuna in oil
   or brine
½ small red onion
75 g (3 oz) frozen peas
400 g (13 oz) leftover
   mashed potatoes
1 tablespoon chopped
   herbs: tarragon, fennel,
   dill or coriander
1 teaspoon mild curry paste
25 g (1 oz) thin corn
   crispbread slices
vegetable oil, for frying
lettuce leaves, to serve

These crispy, crunchy fish cakes are so yummy that they will soon become a family favourite. They are delicious served either with salad or sweetcorn.

1 Tip the tuna into a sieve to drain the oil or brine. Peel and finely chop the onion. Boil the kettle. Put the peas in a small saucepan, cover with the freshly boiled water and cook for 2 minutes. Drain through a sieve.

2 Tip the mashed potatoes into a bowl and add the herbs, curry paste and onion. Mix well with a wooden spoon.

3 Add the tuna and peas and stir gently until all the ingredients are combined, but the tuna stays in slightly chunky pieces. Pat the mixture down in the bowl so it's easy to divide into 4 equal portions. Take a quarter of the mixture and pat it into a cake shape. Make 3 more in the same way so they're all a similar size.

4 Break the crispbread slices into a food processor and whizz to make fine crumbs. Tip the crumbs on to a plate and turn the fish cakes in the crumbs, pressing them gently into each side of the cakes.

5 Pour a thin layer of oil into a large frying pan and heat gently for 1 minute. Using a fish slice, add the fish cakes to the pan and fry gently for about 2 minutes until golden on the underside (check by carefully lifting a fish cake with the fish slice). Turn the fish cakes over and fry again until golden. Use the fish slice to transfer the fish cakes from the pan on to plates and serve with some lettuce leaves.

Toad in the hole

Serves 2 adults and
  2 children
Preparation time 15 minutes
Cooking time 25 minutes

125 g (4 oz) plain flour
small bunch of thyme
1 egg
300 ml (½ pint) milk and
  water mixed
500 g (1 lb) extra-lean pork
  sausages
8 streaky bacon rashers
2 tablespoons sunflower oil
salt and pepper

This traditional hearty dish will give your child a real energy boost and fill up even the hungriest of tummies. Just make sure you buy good-quality bangers.

1 Put the flour and salt and pepper into a large bowl. Tear the leaves off the thyme stems and add 2 tablespoons to the bowl along with the egg. Gradually whisk in the milk and water until the batter is smooth and frothy.

2 Separate the sausages with scissors or a small knife. Stretch each rasher of bacon by placing it on a chopping board and running the flat of the knife along the rasher until it is half as long again. Wrap the bacon around the sausages.

3 Pour the oil into a small roasting tin and add the bacon-wrapped sausages. Place in a preheated oven, 220°C (425°F), Gas Mark 7, and cook for 5 minutes until sizzling. Whisk the batter again.

4 Take the tin out of the oven and quickly pour in the batter. Put the tin back into the oven and cook for about 20 minutes until the batter is well risen and golden. Serve hot with baked beans.

Better than mum's Bolognese

Serves 4
Preparation time 15 minutes
Cooking time 25 minutes

1 onion
3 garlic cloves
3 tablespoons olive oil
500 g (1 lb) lean minced
    beef
2 x 400 g (13 oz) cans
    chopped tomatoes
3 tablespoons sun-dried
    tomato paste or red pesto
150 ml (¼ pint) hot beef or
    chicken stock
1 teaspoon dried oregano
1 teaspoon caster sugar
pinch of salt
250 g (8 oz) linguine pasta
150 g (5 oz) button
    mushrooms

You can use any pasta for this dish, although linguine and spaghetti are probably the most fun to eat. Cook the pasta 'al dente' so it isn't too soft and mushy.

1 Peel the onion and chop it into small pieces. Peel the garlic and press it through a garlic crusher, or finely chop it by hand.

2 Heat 2 tablespoons of the oil in a saucepan and fry the onion for 3 minutes. Add the mince and garlic and fry for 2 minutes, breaking up the beef with a wooden spoon until browned.

3 Add the tomatoes, tomato paste or pesto, stock, oregano, sugar and salt and bring to the boil. Once the sauce is bubbling around the edges, reduce the heat, cover the pan with a lid and cook gently for 20 minutes.

4 While the sauce is cooking, pour plenty of freshly boiled water from the kettle into a large saucepan. Add a little salt and bring to the boil. Carefully lower in the pasta, pushing it down gently as it starts to soften. Cook for about 10 minutes, stirring frequently to break up any bits of pasta that are sticking together.

5 While the linguine is cooking, slice the mushrooms. Heat the remaining oil in a frying pan for 1 minute. Add the mushrooms and fry for about 5 minutes, stirring with a wooden spoon until soft and browned. Stir them into the Bolognese sauce and serve on mounds of linguine.

Spicy tortillas

Serves 2 adults and
2 children
Preparation time 15 minutes
Cooking time 1 hour

1 onion
2 carrots
2 garlic cloves
1 tablespoon olive oil
500 g (1 lb) extra-lean
minced beef
2 teaspoons mild paprika
1 teaspoon ground cumin
415 g (13½ oz) can baked
beans
400 g (13 oz) can chopped
tomatoes
200 ml (7 fl oz) chicken or
beef stock
salt and pepper

For the topping
125 g (4 oz) mixed frozen
vegetables
125 g (4 oz) original tortilla
chips
75 g (3 oz) Cheddar or
mozzarella cheese

Great to share, kids will love this Mexican dish. Don't be afraid to introduce spices into your child's diet – you might be surprised by what she likes.

1 Peel and chop the onion. Peel the carrots with the vegetable peeler and cut into small squares. Peel and crush the garlic.

2 Heat the oil in a medium saucepan and add the mince, onion, carrots and garlic. Fry, stirring with a wooden spoon, until the mince is evenly browned.

3 Stir in the paprika and cumin and cook for 1 minute. Add the baked beans, tomatoes, stock and salt and pepper. Bring to the boil, breaking up any large pieces of mince with the wooden spoon. Cover and cook gently for 45 minutes, stirring from time to time so that it doesn't stick.

4 When the mince is cooked, put the frozen vegetables into a small saucepan, cover with cold water, bring to the boil and cook for 4 minutes. Drain into a sieve.

5 Spoon the mince mixture into a shallow heatproof dish. Sprinkle the vegetables over it and top with the tortilla chips. Grate the cheese and sprinkle over the dish. Cook under a preheated moderate grill until the cheese is bubbling, then spoon on to plates.

Mini beef and bean burgers

Serves 4
Preparation time 15 minutes
Cooking time 10 minutes

225 g (7½ oz) can red
   kidney beans
2 shallots or ½ small onion
400 g (13 oz) lean minced
   beef
1 teaspoon coriander seeds
1 teaspoon cumin seeds
1 teaspoon ground paprika
a little oil, for frying

There's no reason why fast food has to be unhealthy, as these tasty and nutritious burgers prove. Delicious in a bun or with a baked potato.

1   Drain the kidney beans into a sieve and rinse under cold water. Tip the beans into a large bowl and mash them against the sides with a fork so they're broken into smaller pieces.

2   Peel the shallots or onion and chop them into very small pieces. Add to the bowl with the mince.

3   Crush the coriander and cumin seeds using a pestle and mortar until roughly crushed. If you haven't got a pestle and mortar, use a small bowl and the end of a rolling pin to crush the seeds. Add to the bowl of mince with the paprika and mix well. You can use a wooden spoon to do this, but it's much easier with your hands.

4   Turn the mixture out on to a board and divide it into eight equal portions. Using your hands, form each one into a ball and flatten to make a burger shape so they're all a similar size.

5   Heat a thin layer of oil in a frying pan and gently fry the burgers for 5 minutes. If the pan is not big enough, you might need to cook them half at a time. Turn them with a fish slice and fry for a further 5 minutes until they are well browned on the underside (check by carefully lifting a burger with the fish slice). Use the fish slice to transfer the burgers from the pan to a serving plate.

One-pan chicken

Serves 2 adults and
  2 children
Preparation time 15 minutes
Cooking time 1 hour

4 chicken thighs and
  4 chicken drumsticks
1 kg (2 lb) baby new
  potatoes
1 small butternut squash
1 red pepper
1 whole garlic bulb
4 tablespoons olive oil
a few stems of fresh sage or
  a little dried sage
1 teaspoon ground Cajun
  spice
4 teaspoons runny honey
salt and pepper

So easy to make, and so little washing up! To check the chicken is properly cooked, cut into one of the thickest parts and see if the juices run clear.

1 Put the chicken in a colander, rinse with cold water and drain well. On a chopping board, make two or three cuts in each piece of chicken, then put them in a large roasting tin.

2 Wash the potatoes and cut any large ones in half on the washed chopping board. Cut the butternut squash in half lengthways, scoop out the seeds with a spoon and cut the peel away with a vegetable peeler. Cut into thick slices. Cut the red pepper into chunky pieces, discarding the core and seeds. Separate the garlic bulb into cloves but leave their papery skins on.

3 Put all the vegetables into the roasting tin. Spoon over the oil and add the garlic cloves. Sprinkle with a few sage leaves, salt and pepper and Cajun spice.

4 Place the pan in the centre of a preheated oven, 200°C (400°F), Gas Mark 6, and roast for 45 minutes. Carefully take the pan out of the oven. Turn the chicken, spoon the oil over the potatoes and drizzle with the honey. Cook for 15 more minutes until the chicken is thoroughly cooked. To make sure the chicken is cooked, make a cut in one of the thickest parts. The meat should look the same colour throughout with no hint of pink juices.

Chicken dippers with salsa

Serves 2 adults and
2 children

Preparation time 20 minutes

Cooking time 5–6 minutes

4 boneless skinless chicken
breasts, about 625 g
(1¼ lb) in total
2 eggs
2 tablespoons milk
100 g (3½ oz) bread
4 tablespoons ready grated
Parmesan cheese
25 g (1 oz) butter
2 tablespoons sunflower oil
salt and pepper

For the salsa
2 tomatoes
¼ cucumber
75 g (3 oz) canned
sweetcorn
a few stems of fresh
coriander

Fast food that is not only fun to make but tastes scrummy. Your child will love getting messy while dipping the chicken in egg and coating it in breadcrumbs.

1 Put the chicken into a colander, rinse with cold water and drain well. On a chopping board, cut the chicken into long, finger-like slices.

2 Using a fork, beat together the eggs, milk and a little salt and pepper in a shallow bowl.

3 Tear the bread into pieces and whizz in a food processor or blender until fine crumbs, then tip the crumbs into another shallow bowl and mix with the Parmesan.

4 Dip one chicken strip into the egg, then roll it in the breadcrumbs. Repeat until all chicken strips are coated.

5 For the salsa, on the washed chopping board, cut the tomatoes and cucumber into tiny pieces about the size of the sweetcorn. Mix the three vegetables in another bowl. Snip some of the coriander into pieces with scissors and mix 1 tablespoon into the tomato mixture.

6 Heat the butter and oil in a large frying pan, add the chicken, a few pieces at a time, until they are all added. Cook for 5–6 minutes, turning several times until evenly browned. (Cook in two batches if the pan is not very big.) Arrange the chicken on serving plates with spoonfuls of the salsa.

Perfect
puds

Warm plum sundaes

Serves 4
Preparation time 20 minutes
Cooking time 8 minutes

500 g (1 lb) red plums
100 g (3½ oz) golden caster
  sugar
15g (½ oz) cornflour
1 teaspoon vanilla extract
3 egg yolks
250 ml (8 fl oz) milk
150 ml (¼ pint) double
  cream
1 tablespoon toasted
  almonds
icing sugar, for dusting

A great alternative to ice cream sundaes, sweet stewed plums topped with luscious custard will have the whole family fighting over this truly scrumptious pudding.

1 Cut the plums into quarters, discarding the stones. Put them in a small saucepan with 75 g (3 oz) of the sugar and 2 tablespoons water. Cover the pan and heat very gently for about 5 minutes or until the plums are tender but not falling apart. Tip the plums into a sieve set over a bowl to catch the juices and leave to stand while making the custard.

2 Whisk the remaining sugar with the cornflour, vanilla extract and egg yolks in a heatproof bowl. Pour the milk into the cleaned saucepan and bring just to the boil. As the milk starts to rise up in the pan, remove it from the heat and pour it over the mixture in the bowl, whisking well.

3 Carefully tip the custard back into the pan and heat gently, stirring well until thickened and bubbling. Remove the custard from the heat and turn it into the bowl. Leave to stand for 10 minutes.

4 Divide the plums among 4 glasses and add a tablespoonful of the juice to each. Using a balloon whisk, whip the cream with the remaining plum juices until slightly thickened. Stir in the custard until smooth and spoon over the plums. Scatter each dish with toasted almonds and dust with icing sugar through a small sieve (or tea strainer), then serve.

Chocolate puddle pudding

Serves 4–6
Preparation time 15 minutes
Cooking time 20–25 minutes

This magical rich dessert goes into the oven with the sauce on top, and comes out with the sponge on top. Ask the kids to explain that mystery to you!

75 g (3 oz) soft margarine
   or softened butter
75 g (3 oz) soft light brown
   sugar
65 g (2½ oz) self-raising
   flour
3 tablespoons cocoa
   powder
3 eggs
½ teaspoon baking powder
little icing sugar, to finish

For the sauce
2 tablespoons cocoa
   powder
50 g (2 oz) soft light brown
   sugar
250 ml (8 fl oz) boiling
   water

1   To make the sauce, put the cocoa and sugar into a small bowl and use a wooden spoon to mix in a little of the measured boiling water to make a smooth paste. Gradually mix in the rest of the boiling water.

2   To make the pudding, rub a little of the margarine or butter all over the base and sides of a 1.2 litre (2 pint) ovenproof glass soufflé dish or pie dish. Stand the dish on a baking sheet. Put all the other ingredients, except the icing sugar, into another bowl and beat together with a wooden spoon or electric mixer until smooth.

3   Spoon the pudding mixture into the dish, spread the top level, then pour the cocoa sauce over the top. Place in the centre of a preheated oven, 180°C (350°F), Gas Mark 4, and bake for 20–25 minutes until the sauce has sunk to the bottom of the dish and the pudding is well risen. (The deeper the dish, the longer it will take for the pudding to cook.)

4   To finish, sift a little icing sugar on to the pudding and serve with scoops of vanilla ice cream or a little pouring cream.

Easy orange cheesecake

Serves 6
Preparation time 20
minutes, plus chilling

150 g (5 oz) **digestive**
biscuits
50 g (2 oz) **butter**
2 tablespoons **golden syrup**
312 g (10½ oz) can
mandarin oranges in
natural juice
250 g (8 oz) **tub**
mascarpone cheese
150 g (5 oz) **virtually fat-free**
fromage frais
50 g (2 oz) **caster sugar**
1 small **orange**
1 **lime**
150 ml (¼ pint) **double**
cream

Kids will love the contrasting crunchiness of the base and the creaminess of the tangy cheesecake mix. For a zingier taste, use a small lemon instead of the orange.

1 Put the biscuits into a plastic bag, seal and bash with a rolling pin until the biscuits become fine crumbs. Heat the butter and syrup in a small saucepan until melted, stir in the biscuit crumbs using a wooden spoon and mix well.

2 Tip the crumb mixture into the base of a 20 cm (8 inch) springform tin and press flat.

3 Open the can of mandarin oranges and tip into a sieve to drain off the juice. Arrange about three-quarters of them over the crumbs in the tin. Keep the rest for decorating the cheesecake.

4 Put the mascarpone cheese into a mixing bowl and mix with a wooden spoon to soften it. Stir in the fromage frais and sugar. Take the rind off the orange and lime using a zester or the fine holes on a grater, then cut the fruits in half and squeeze out the juice. Stir the rind and juice into the cheese mixture.

5 Use a hand or electric whisk to whip the cream in another bowl until it thickens and becomes soft swirls. Gently fold into the cheese mixture.

6 Pour the mixture into the tin and make soft, wave-like shapes over the top with the back of a metal spoon. Decorate with the remaining mandarins then chill the cheesecake in the refrigerator for at least 4 hours.

7 To serve, run a thin-bladed knife around the edge of the cheesecake. Unclip the tin and transfer the cheesecake to a serving plate.

Ice dream

Serves 4–5
Preparation time 20 minutes

300 ml (½ pint) double
  cream
250 g (8 oz) frozen summer
  fruits, such as
  strawberries, raspberries,
  blackcurrants and
  cherries
50 g (2 oz) icing sugar
extra fresh fruit, such as
  strawberries or
  raspberries, to decorate
sugar sprinkles, to decorate
  (optional)

What child doesn't like ice cream? And by making their own you know there are no artificial flavours or additives (until they add the toppings anyway!).

1 Pour 100 ml (3½ fl oz) of the cream into a small bowl. Tip the frozen fruit into a food processor and add the icing sugar. Blend very lightly until the fruit starts to break up.

2 With the machine running, gradually pour the remaining cream into the processor through the funnel until the ice cream is thick and smooth. (If the frozen mixture clogs together and doesn't whizz around, turn the machine off and stir the fruit and cream to break it up.) Put the processor bowl in the freezer while you whip the cream.

3 Whisk the reserved cream until it is only just peaking when the whisk is lifted from the bowl. Spoon half the cream into 4–5 serving glasses.

4 Spoon the ice cream on top of the cream and then finish each pud with another blob of cream. Scatter with a few fresh fruits and serve scattered with sugar sprinkles, if you like.

Warm summer fruit trifle

Serves 6
Preparation time 15 minutes
Cooking time 20 minutes

This great-looking pudding is extremely simple to make. To ring the changes, use cooked apples and blackberries or a can of cherry pie filling instead.

100 g (3½ oz) trifle sponges, plain sponge, Madeira cake or jam Swiss roll
3 tablespoons orange juice, freshly squeezed or from a carton
375 g (12 oz) frozen mixed summer fruits, just defrosted
425 g (14 oz) can custard
3 egg whites
75 g (3 oz) caster sugar

1 Crumble the sponge into the base of a 1.2 litre (2 pint) ovenproof soufflé or pie dish. Drizzle the orange juice over the sponge. Add the mixed fruits. Spoon the can of custard over the top.

2 Put the egg whites into a large bowl. With an electric whisk, whisk until the eggs fill the bowl and the bowl can be turned upside down without them falling out. Gradually whisk in the sugar, a spoonful at a time. Whisk for a minute or two more once all the sugar has been added until the egg mixture looks smooth and glossy.

3 Spoon the egg mixture over the top of the custard and leave the top in large swirls. Place in the centre of a preheated oven, 160°C (325°F), Gas Mark 3, and cook for 20 minutes until the meringue is golden brown on the top and all the trifle layers are heated through.

Watermelon lollies

Serves 6
Preparation time 15 minutes,
plus freezing

These colourful lollies are delightfully refreshing. You can use the same recipe to make papaya, mango or peach lollies, just remove the seeds or stones before pureéing.

625 g (1¼ lb) wedge of watermelon
2 limes
150 ml (¼ pint) apple juice
2 tablespoons caster sugar

1 Using a large metal spoon, scoop the red melon flesh and black seeds away from the green skin and place in a food processor or liquidizer. Blend briefly so that the fruit is puréed but the seeds are still whole.

2 Tip the mixture into a sieve set over a large bowl and press the red melon flesh through the sieve with a metal spoon, leaving the seeds behind in the sieve.

3 Finely grate the rind of the limes and add to the melon purée. Cut the limes in half and squeeze out the juice. Stir into the melon purée with the apple juice and sugar.

4 Pour the melon mixture into sections of a plastic ice lolly mould. Add the lids. Freeze for 4 hours, or longer if you have time, until frozen solid.

5 To take the lollies out of the moulds, dip the plastic mould into a bowl of just boiled water from the kettle. Count to 10, then lift each lolly and its top out of the mould and serve.

Kiwi meringue gâteau

Makes 8 slices
Preparation time 25 minutes
Cooking time 1¼ hours

4 egg whites
125 g (4 oz) caster sugar
100 g (3½ oz) light muscovado sugar
1 teaspoon cornflour
1 teaspoon white wine vinegar

To finish
4 kiwi fruit
150 g (5 oz) seedless grapes
300 ml (½ pint) double cream

This fruit-filled stacked pavlova is sure to be a big hit at a summer party, and also looks great when filled with berries.

1 Line 2 baking sheets with pieces of nonstick baking paper and draw a 23 cm (9 inch) circle on one and an 18 cm (7 inch) circle on the other, using cake tins as templates to draw around.

2 Put the egg whites in a large bowl and whisk using an electric whisk until very stiff. To test whether they are ready, turn the bowl upside down – if the eggs look like they may slide out, whisk for a few minutes more. Gradually whisk in the sugars, a teaspoonful at a time, and continue whisking for 1–2 minutes more, even when all the sugar has been added, so that the meringue is very thick and glossy. Mix the cornflour and vinegar in a cup, then whisk into the meringue.

3 Spoon the meringue on to the lined baking sheets and spread within the marked circles. Place in a preheated oven, 110°C (225°F), Gas Mark ¼, and bake for 1¼ hours or until they can be lifted easily off the paper. Leave to cool on the paper. Don't worry if the meringues crack slightly.

4 To finish the gâteau, peel the brown skin away from the kiwi fruit and discard, then cut the fruit into slices. Cut the grapes in half. Whip the cream in a bowl using the cleaned whisk until the cream has thickened and makes soft swirls.

5 Lift the larger meringue off its lining paper and put on a serving plate. Spread with the cream and arrange the fruit on top. Add the other meringue layer and store the gâteau in the refrigerator until needed – it is best eaten on the day it is made.

Cakes

Coconut and raspberry cup cakes

Makes 12

Preparation time 15 minutes

Cooking time 20 minutes

125 g (4 oz) butter

75 g (3 oz) self-raising flour

200 g (7 oz) icing sugar

50 g (2 oz) desiccated coconut

4 egg whites

200 g (7 oz) fresh raspberries

Surprisingly easy to make, these delicious cup cakes are studded with clusters of succulent fresh raspberries but could be made just as well with blueberries.

1   Line a 12-cup muffin tin with paper cases.

2   Put the butter in a small saucepan and melt over a low heat. Meanwhile, sift the flour and icing sugar into a large mixing bowl, add the coconut and stir together.

3   Add the egg whites and mix together, then add the melted butter and stir again until combined into a thick batter.

4   Tip the batter into a measuring jug and pour into the prepared muffin cases, filling each one about half full. Place a few raspberries on the top of each cake.

5   Place the cakes in a preheated oven, 180°C (350°F), Gas Mark 4, and bake for 20 minutes or until they are golden and springy to the touch. Remove them from the oven and allow to cool for a few minutes in the tin then transfer them to a wire rack.

Triple choc brownies

Makes 18
Preparation time 20 minutes
Cooking time 20–25 minutes

150 g (5 oz) dark chocolate
125 g (4 oz) butter, at room
temperature
75 g (3 oz) white chocolate
75 g (3 oz) milk chocolate
3 eggs
200 g (7 oz) caster sugar
150 g (5 oz) self-raising flour
1 teaspoon baking powder

Everyone will adore these gooey brownies. For a change, melt the white chocolate and drizzle it over the top of the cooked brownies instead of adding it to the mixture.

1   Line a small roasting tin with nonstick baking paper, by cutting the paper a little larger than the tin, then snip into the corners and press the paper into the tin.

2   Half-fill a medium saucepan with water, bring just to the boil, then turn off the heat and place a large bowl on top. Break the dark chocolate into pieces and cut the butter into pieces on the plate, then add both to the bowl. Leave for 5 minutes or so until melted.

3   Put the white and milk chocolate in a plastic bag and hit with a rolling pin until broken into small pieces.

4   Whisk the eggs and sugar together in another bowl for 5 minutes using an electric whisk until thick and very frothy.

5   Pour the melted chocolate and butter mixture over the top and mix in very gently using a metal spoon. Sift the flour and baking powder over the top, then carefully fold in.

6   Pour the mixture into the lined tin. Sprinkle the white and milk chocolate pieces over the top. Place the cake in a preheated oven, 180°C (350°F), Gas Mark 4, and bake for 20–25 minutes until the top is crusty and the centre still wobbles slightly. Leave to cool and harden in the tin.

7   Lift the paper and cake out of the tin, remove the paper and put the cake on a chopping board. Cut the cake into 18 pieces. The brownies can be stored in an airtight tin for up to 2 days.

Mini birthday cake squares

Makes 24
Preparation time 20 minutes
Cooking time 25–30 minutes

A fun alternative to a traditional birthday cake, you could even let everyone at your child's birthday party decorate their own cake ... if you can cope with the mess!

a little cooking oil, for
  greasing
250 g (8 oz) soft margarine
250 g (8 oz) caster sugar
250 g (8 oz) self-raising
  flour
4 eggs
grated rind of 1 lemon or 1
  small orange

To decorate
100 g (3½ oz) butter, at
  room temperature
200 g (7 oz) icing sugar
2–4 teaspoons milk
a few drops blue, orange
  and pink food colouring
24 candles and candle-
  holders
selection of sweets (such as
  dolly mixtures, mini
  candy-coated chocolate
  sweets or mini
  marshmallows)
sugar strands or hundreds
  and thousands

1 Using a pastry brush, grease a small roasting tin with a little oil, line the base with a rectangle of greaseproof paper and brush this with a little extra oil.

2 Put all the cake ingredients into a large bowl and beat with a wooden spoon. Spoon into the tin and smooth flat.

3 Place the cake in a preheated oven, 180°C (350°F), Gas Mark 4, and bake for 25–30 minutes until it is well risen and golden brown, and the top springs back when lightly pressed. Leave the cake to cool in the tin for about 10 minutes, then loosen the sides with a round-bladed knife and turn it out on to a wire rack. Carefully remove the lining paper and leave the cake to cool completely.

4 To make the icing, beat the butter in a medium bowl with a little of the icing sugar (there is no need to sift it first), then gradually mix in the rest, a few spoonfuls at a time, with enough milk to make a smooth, spreadable icing. Divide the icing into three and place in separate small bowls. Colour one-third of the icing pale blue, one-third pale orange and the rest pale pink.

5 Put the cake on a large chopping board and cut it into 3 pieces. Spread a different coloured icing over each piece of cake using a round-bladed knife. Cut each iced cake into 8 small pieces with a large sharp knife. Place a candle-holder and candle in the centre of each piece, then arrange the sweets and sugar strands around it. Store in an airtight tin for up to 2 days.

Mini iced gingerbread

Makes 12
Preparation time 20 minutes
Cooking time 10–15 minutes

Kids adore decorating these tasty buns with sweets and icing, which you could make in different colours. The gingerbreads also make very charming presents when beautifully wrapped.

125 g (4 oz) butter
250 g (8 oz) golden syrup
75 g (3 oz) dark muscovado sugar
250 g (8 oz) self-raising flour
1 teaspoon ground ginger
1 teaspoon mixed spice
½ teaspoon bicarbonate of soda
150 ml (¼ pint) milk
2 eggs
125 g (4 oz) icing sugar
few sliced red, green and yellow glacé cherries or sweets
Cellophane and ribbon, to finish

1   Line a deep 12-cup muffin tin with paper cases.

2   Put the butter, syrup and sugar into a saucepan. Heat the pan gently, stirring with a wooden spoon, until the butter has completely melted.

3   Take the pan off the heat. Sift the flour, spices and bicarbonate into a bowl. Beat the milk and eggs together in a jug with a fork. Add the dry ingredients to the pan, mix with a wooden spoon, then gradually beat in the milk mixture until smooth.

4   Half-fill the jug with the gingerbread mixture, then pour it into the muffin cases until two-thirds full. Refill the jug and continue until all the cases are filled. Place the cakes in the centre of a preheated oven, 180°C (350°F), Gas Mark 4, and bake for 10–15 minutes until well risen and the tops spring back when pressed with your fingertips. Cool in the tin.

5   Sift the icing sugar into another bowl. Gradually mix in 4 teaspoons of water until a smooth thick icing. Arrange the cherries or sweets over the cakes and drizzle over the icing from a spoon in squiggly lines. Leave to set, then wrap individually in Cellophane and tie with ribbon.

Butterfly cakes

Makes 12
Preparation time 20 minutes
Cooking time 20 minutes

Butterfly cakes are traditional children's party fare, an easy, one-bowl mix your kids will love to make. Try varying the colour of the icing or add sugar strands and sweets.

100 g (3½ oz) butter or
    margarine, at room
    temperature
100 g (3½ oz) caster sugar
2 drops vanilla extract
2 eggs
100 g (3½ oz) self-raising
    flour
icing sugar, for dusting
icing pens, to decorate
    (optional)

For the icing
50 g (2 oz) butter, at room
    temperature
125 g (4 oz) icing sugar,
    sifted
2–3 drops food colouring
    (optional)
1 tablespoon milk or water

1   Line a 12-cup patty tin with paper cases.

2   Place the butter, sugar and vanilla extract in a large mixing bowl and beat together with a wooden spoon or electric whisk until smooth and creamy. Break the eggs into the mixture one at a time, being careful not to let any shell fall in. Beat the mixture again between egg additions.

3   Place a sieve over the mixing bowl, sift in the flour, then stir it in. Drop dessertspoonfuls of the mixture into the prepared cases.

4   Place the cakes in a preheated oven, 180°C (350°F), Gas Mark 4, and bake for 20 minutes or until golden and springy to the touch. Remove the cakes from the oven and allow to cool in the tin for a few minutes then transfer to a wire rack and allow to cool completely.

5   Meanwhile, make the butter icing. Place the ingredients in a bowl and beat together, then leave in a cool place while the cakes are cooling.

6   Using a teaspoon, dig out a circle about 2.5 cm (1 inch) in diameter from the top of each cake. Slice the cone-like piece of cake you have removed in half.

7   Fill the holes in the cakes with the icing, then gently stick the two halves of each cone back into the icing so that they stick up like a butterfly perched on top. Dust with icing sugar and/or decorate with icing pens.

Strawberry and mascarpone layer cake

Makes 8 slices
Preparation time 20 minutes
Cooking time 20 minutes

A good excuse to invite friends round for tea. This delicious cake is best eaten the day it is made, but it probably won't last much longer than that anyway!

a little cooking oil, for
   greasing
175 g (6 oz) soft margarine
175 g (6 oz) caster sugar
175 g (6 oz) self-raising flour
1 teaspoon baking powder
grated rind of 1 lemon
3 eggs

To finish
175 g (6 oz) low-fat
   mascarpone cheese
2 tablespoons icing sugar,
   plus extra for dusting
400 g (13 oz) strawberries,
   stalks removed
3 tablespoons strawberry
   jam

1 Brush two 20 cm (8 inch) Victoria sandwich tins with a little oil, line the bases with circles of greaseproof paper and brush these with a little extra oil.

2 Put all the cake ingredients in a large bowl and beat with a wooden spoon. Divide the mixture equally between the lined tins and smooth flat with the back of a metal spoon.

3 Place the tins in a preheated oven, 180°C (350°F), Gas Mark 4, and bake the cakes for about 20 minutes until they are well risen and golden brown, and the tops spring back when lightly pressed. Leave the cakes to cool in the tins for 5 minutes, then loosen the sides with a round-bladed knife and turn out on to a wire rack. Remove the lining paper and leave to cool completely.

4 To make the filling, put the mascarpone and icing sugar in a medium bowl and beat together until soft.

5 Put one of the cakes on a serving plate and spread with the cheese mixture. Reserve 4 strawberries for the decoration and slice the rest. Mix these with the jam in a small bowl, then spoon on top of the cheese mixture. Carefully put the second cake on top. Decorate with the reserved strawberries, cut in halves (keeping them in place with a little mascarpone, if necessary) and a little extra sifted icing sugar.

Chocolate and orange swirl cake

Makes 10 slices
Preparation time 25 minutes
Cooking time 35–40 minutes

a little cooking oil, for
   greasing
4 teaspoons cocoa powder
4 teaspoons boiling water
175 g (6 oz) soft margarine
175 g (6 oz) caster sugar
200 g (7 oz) self-raising
   flour
3 eggs
grated rind of ½ orange
sugar flowers, to decorate

For the icing
50 g (2 oz) butter
25 g (1 oz) cocoa powder
250 g (8 oz) icing sugar
1–2 tablespoons milk

This is a fun cake to make and it looks absolutely fantastic when it is decorated.

1   Lightly brush a 20 cm (8 inch) round springform cake tin with a little oil, line the base with a circle of greaseproof paper and brush this with a little extra oil.

2   Put the cocoa powder in a small bowl, add the boiling water and mix to a paste.

3   Put the margarine, sugar, flour and eggs in a large mixing bowl and beat with a wooden spoon until smooth. Spoon half the mixture into a medium bowl and stir in the cocoa paste. Stir the orange rind into the other half of the cake mixture.

4   Add alternate spoonfuls of the 2 mixtures to the tin then run a round-bladed knife through the colours to swirl them together. Place in a preheated oven, 180°C (350°F), Gas Mark 4. Bake the cake for 35–40 minutes until it is well risen and golden brown. Leave it to cool in the tin for 15 minutes, then transfer to a wire rack. Remove the lining paper and leave to cool.

5   Put the butter in a saucepan and heat until melted. Stir in the cocoa powder and cook for 1 minute. Take off the heat and stir in the icing sugar. Return to the hob and heat for 1 minute until glossy. Stir in enough milk to make a smooth, spreadable icing. Transfer the cake to a wire rack set over a large plate. Spoon the icing over the top, then smooth evenly with a knife. Decorate with sugar flowers and leave to harden for 30 minutes before slicing. Store in an airtight tin for up to 2 days.

Peach melba cake

Makes 10–12 slices

Preparation time 30 minutes

Cooking time 1 hour 10 minutes–1 hour 25 minutes

oil, for greasing

3 peaches, about 375 g (12 oz) in total

200 g (7 oz) butter, at room temperature

200 g (7 oz) caster sugar

grated rind of 1 lemon

3 eggs

200 g (7 oz) self-raising flour

125 g (4 oz) raspberries

150 g (5 oz) full-fat cream cheese

sifted icing sugar, to decorate

This luscious cake, packed to the brim with raspberries, peaches and cream, is guaranteed to impress everyone who samples it, whatever their age.

1 Brush a 20 cm (8 inch) round springform tin with a little oil, line the base with greaseproof paper and brush this with a little extra oil. Cut the peaches in half, cut out the stones, then thinly slice the fruit.

2 Beat the butter, sugar and lemon rind in a large bowl with a wooden spoon until fluffy. Beat the eggs in a small bowl with a fork. Slowly add a little egg to the butter mixture then some flour, beating well after each addition. Continue until both have been added. Mix for 1–2 minutes. Spoon half the cake mixture into the lined tin and smooth flat.

3 Cover the cake with half the peach slices and half the raspberries then dot all the cream cheese over the top, using the teaspoon. Spoon the rest of the cake mixture on top and gently smooth flat. Arrange the remaining peach slices and raspberries over the top.

4 Bake the cake in a preheated oven, 160°C (325°F), Gas Mark 3, for about 1 hour 10 minutes to 1 hour 25 minutes until it is well risen and a skewer comes out cleanly when pushed into the centre. Leave the cake to cool in the tin for 15 minutes. Loosen the sides with a round-bladed knife, then release the cake and transfer it to a wire rack. Remove the lining paper and leave the cake to cool completely. To serve, dust the cake with a little sifted icing sugar.

Biscuits
and
cookies

Chocolate chip cookies

Makes about 24
Preparation time 10 minutes
Cooking time 10–15 minutes

These chunky, chocolate-chip-laden cookies are fast and fun to make. Ideal to give your kids a quick energy boost, they will soon disappear out of the biscuit jar.

100 g (3½ oz) **butter or margarine, at room temperature**
100 g (3½ oz) **soft light brown sugar**
1 **egg**
1 teaspoon **vanilla extract**
150 g (5 oz) **self-raising flour**
75 g (3 oz) **porridge oats**
50 g (2 oz) **plain or milk chocolate drops**
50 g (2 oz) **white chocolate drops**

1 Line 2 baking sheets with nonstick baking paper.

2 Place the butter and sugar in a large mixing bowl and beat them together until creamy using an electric whisk or a wooden spoon.

3 Add the egg and vanilla extract and mix again. Place a sieve over the mixing bowl, sift in the flour and then stir it in.

4 Add the oats and chocolate drops and stir in, then, using a teaspoon and a finger to scrape the mixture off, place generous spoonfuls of the mixture in 24 or so lumpy heaps on the baking sheets. Allow plenty of space between the heaps as the cookies will spread as they cook.

5 Place the cookies in a preheated oven, 190°C (375°F), Gas Mark 5, and bake them for about 10 minutes, until the ones on the top shelf are golden brown, then remove them from the oven and move the other baking sheet up from the bottom shelf. Bake these for a further 3–5 minutes until they are golden, then remove from the oven.

6 Leave the cookies to cool on the baking sheets for a few minutes then transfer, with a fish slice or palette knife, to a wire rack. The cookies will crisp up as they cool.

Chocolate crackles

Makes 12
Preparation time 15 minutes,
  plus chilling
Cooking time 3–4 minutes

**15 g (½ oz) unsalted butter,
  plus a little extra for
  greasing**
**50 g (2 oz) blanched
  almonds**
150 g (5 oz) milk chocolate
50 g (2 oz) sultanas
75 g (3 oz) crispy rice cereal
25 g (1 oz) white chocolate

The dried fruit and nuts add a great texture and flavour, but you can leave these out if your children prefer them plain.

1 Use a little butter to lightly grease the base and sides of a 20 cm (8 inch) round, shallow loose-bottomed cake tin. This will stop the crackles sticking to the tin.

2 Chop the almonds and lightly toast them, either on a foil-lined grill pan under the grill, or by stirring them in a frying pan without any oil until they are lightly coloured. Transfer to a plate to drain.

3 Break the milk chocolate into a heatproof bowl and add the butter. Place the bowl over a pan of gently simmering water, set it over the lowest heat until the chocolate has melted. Make sure the base of the bowl isn't in contact with the water or the chocolate will overheat. Once the chocolate has melted, use oven gloves to lift the bowl carefully from the pan.

4 Stir the sultanas, almonds and cereal into the chocolate until coated. Tip into the greased tin and pack down firmly with the back of a dessertspoon.

5 Break the white chocolate into pieces and melt in a heatproof bowl over a pan of simmering water. Using a teaspoon, drizzle the chocolate over the cake to decorate. Chill the cake in the refrigerator for at least 20 minutes, then cut it into wedges.

Noah's ark cookies

Makes 20
Preparation time 20 minutes
Cooking time 10 minutes

Children will enjoy cutting out and decorating these delightful animal shapes, so make sure you have a good selection of coloured icings, sweets and other edible decorations.

**175 g (6 oz) butter, at room
    temperature**
75 g (3 oz) caster sugar
275 g (9 oz) plain flour

To decorate
**tubes of different coloured
    writing icing**
**mini candy-coated
    chocolate sweets**

1   Cut the butter into small pieces on a plate, then put it into a large mixing bowl with the sugar and flour. Rub the butter into the flour mixture between your fingertips to make tiny crumbs, or use an electric mixer. Using your hands, squeeze the cookie crumbs together to make a dough. Knead lightly, then cut in half.

2   Place one of the pieces of cookie dough between 2 large sheets of nonstick baking paper, then roll it out thinly. Peel off the top piece of paper and stamp out animal shapes using a selection of different cookie cutters, making 2 of each animal shape.

3   Carefully lift the cookie animals with a palette knife and place on ungreased baking sheets. Add the cookie trimmings to the other half of the cookie dough and squeeze together back into a ball. Continue rolling and stamping out the mixture until it has all been shaped into animals.

4   Place the cookies in a preheated oven, 180°C (350°F), Gas Mark 4, and bake for about 10 minutes until they are pale golden. Leave to cool on the baking sheets, or transfer to a wire rack if preferred.

5   When the cookies are cold, let your imagination run riot as you add the animal markings, piping features with tubes of coloured icing and adding sweets for eyes. Set the cookies aside for 30 minutes for the icing to harden before serving. They can be stored in an airtight tin for up to 2 days.

Chocolate kisses

Makes 10
Preparation time 20 minutes
Cooking time 10 minutes

100 g (3½ oz) butter, at room temperature
50 g (2 oz) caster sugar
2 tablespoons cocoa powder
150 g (5 oz) self-raising flour

For the filling
50 g (2 oz) butter, at room temperature
100 g (3½ oz) icing sugar
a few drops peppermint essence
a few drops green and pink food colouring (optional)

As these biscuits are so simple to make let your child experiment with different shapes and icings or even different fillings like peanut butter. Hours of amusement!

1 Put the butter and caster sugar in a large bowl and beat with a wooden spoon or electric mixer until light and fluffy. Sift in the cocoa powder and flour and mix together until smooth, squeezing with your hands when the dough becomes too stiff to stir.

2 Take teaspoonfuls of the dough, roll into 20 balls and put on ungreased baking sheets, leaving a little space in between to allow them to spread during cooking. Flatten the cookies slightly with the back of a fork.

3 Place the cookies in a preheated oven, 180°C (350°F), Gas Mark 4, and bake for 10 minutes until they are lightly browned. Leave to cool on the baking sheets.

4 Meanwhile, make the filling by beating together the butter, icing sugar and peppermint essence in a small bowl until smooth. Spoon half the filling into another bowl and, if you like, mix a few drops of green food colouring into one half and a little pink food colouring into the rest in the other bowl. Spread 5 of the cookies with the green filling and 5 with the pink, then top with the remaining cookies. The cookies can be stored in an airtight tin for up to 2 days.

Chocolate tree decorations

Makes 22
Preparation time 20 minutes
Cooking time 10–12 minutes

Making Christmas decorations with your children is a lovely way to get into the festive spirit, and these homemade decorations will look fabulous on any tree.

a little cooking oil, for greasing
75 g (3 oz) butter
3 tablespoons golden syrup
150 g (5 oz) caster sugar
325 g (11 oz) plain flour
15 g (½ oz) cocoa
1 teaspoon ground cinnamon
2 teaspoons bicarbonate of soda
4 tablespoons milk

To decorate
1 tube ready-to-use white writing icing
mini candy-coated chocolate drops or other tiny sweets
fine ribbon, to finish

1 Brush 2 baking sheets with oil, using a pastry brush. Put the butter, syrup and sugar in a saucepan. Heat gently, stirring with a wooden spoon, until the butter has melted.

2 Sift the flour, cocoa, cinnamon and bicarbonate of soda into a bowl, then add to the melted butter mixture with the milk. Mix to a smooth ball. Leave for 5 minutes or until cool enough to handle.

3 Knead until evenly coloured, then roll out on a lightly floured surface until it is 5 mm (¼ inch) thick. Stamp out Christmas shapes using large Christmas tree cutters (or other festive shapes), then transfer to the baking sheets. Re-roll the trimmings and continue cutting shapes until all the dough is used. (If the dough gets too stiff to re-roll the trimmings, warm it in the microwave on Full Power for 20–30 seconds, depending on the amount of dough.)

4 Place the biscuits in a preheated oven, 180°C (350°F), Gas Mark 4, and bake for 10–12 minutes until just beginning to darken. Make a hole in the top of each biscuit with the end of a teaspoon, then leave to cool on the sheets.

5 Pipe on white icing to decorate by squeezing the icing straight from the tube. Decorate with sweets and leave to harden. Thread fine ribbon through the hole at the top of each biscuit, then tie to the Christmas tree. Eat within 3 days.

Gingerbread kings and queens

Makes about 12
Preparation time 30 minutes, plus chilling
Cooking time 10–15 minutes

100 g (3½ oz) butter or margarine, at room temperature
100 g (3½ oz) caster sugar
1 egg
few drops vanilla extract
200 g (7 oz) self-raising flour, plus extra for dusting
1 tablespoon ground ginger

To decorate
small sweets
icing pens
cake decorations

Let your child be creative when decorating these figures – brilliant cookies that all the family can have fun making. By the end they will undoubtedly look too good to eat!

1 Line 2 large baking sheets with nonstick baking paper.

2 Place the butter and sugar in a large mixing bowl and beat until creamy. Crack the egg into the mixture. Add the vanilla extract and mix again until smooth.

3 Sift the flour and ginger into the mixing bowl, then stir with a wooden spoon to make a soft dough. Using your hands, pull all the bits together into a ball. If the dough is very sticky, add a little more flour.

4 Wrap the dough in clingfilm and chill it in the refrigerator for 1 hour. When chilled, dust a work surface with flour and roll or press out the dough with your fingers until it is about 5 mm (¼ inch) thick. Using gingerbread men and women cutters, cut out shapes from the dough and transfer to the prepared baking sheets using a palette knife.

5 Place the biscuits in a preheated oven, 180°C (350°F), Gas Mark 4, and bake for 10–15 minutes, or until pale golden. Transfer to a wire rack and leave to cool.

6 When the gingerbread figures are cool, decorate them using sweetie jewels, icing pens and cake decorations.

Cobweb biscuits

Makes about 30
Preparation time 30
  minutes, plus chilling
Cooking time 8–10 minutes

**200 g (7 oz) butter, cold, cut
  into small pieces**
**275 g (9 oz) plain flour, plus
  extra for dusting**
100 g (3½ oz) icing sugar
2 teaspoons vanilla extract

For the icing
125 g (4 oz) icing sugar
**1 tablespoon preboiled
  warm water**
black icing pen
**small spider sweets or cake
  decorations**

A spooky creation to make for Halloween. These scrummy cookies are what's known as refrigerator biscuits as the mixture is chilled until firm enough to slice very thinly.

1 Line a baking sheet with nonstick baking paper.

2 Put the butter into a large mixing bowl, sift in the flour and rub the butter into the flour with your fingertips until the mixture resembles fine breadcrumbs. Stir in the icing sugar and vanilla extract and squish the mixture together with your hands until it comes together into a ball.

3 Tip the mixture out on to a lightly floured work surface and squidge it together with your hands and then shape and roll it into a long sausage shape. Wrap in clingfilm or baking paper and chill for at least an hour.

4 Remove the clingfilm or baking paper from the dough and slice it as thinly as possible. Place these slices on the prepared baking sheet.

5 Place the biscuits in a preheated oven, 200°C (400°F), Gas Mark 6, and bake them for 8–10 minutes or until they are a light golden brown. Leave to cool on the baking sheet for 5 minutes, then transfer to a wire rack to cool completely.

6 Meanwhile, make the glacé icing by sifting the icing sugar into a bowl, then add the water and stir it in. Add more water drop by drop until you have a thick icing that coats the back of the spoon.

7 When the biscuits are cool, use a teaspoon to coat each with white icing. Then take the black icing pen and draw on a simple cobweb design. Draw or stick little spiders on to the webs, then allow to set before serving.

Christmas garlands

Makes 6
Preparation time 30 minutes
Cooking time 15 minutes

These garlands are fun to make and, if you don't want to eat them, they can be used as table decorations or hung by ribbons from the Christmas tree.

50 g (2 oz) butter
150 g (5 oz) plain flour
50 g (2 oz) caster sugar,
    plus a little for sprinkling
finely grated rind of a
    small lemon
1 egg, beaten
pieces of angelica and
    glacé cherries, to
    decorate

1 Line 2 baking sheets with nonstick baking paper.

2 Put the butter in a bowl, sift in the flour and rub the ingredients together between your thumbs and fingers until the mixture resembles fine breadcrumbs.

3 Add the sugar and lemon rind and stir everything together with a wooden spoon. Add most of the egg and stir again until the mixture comes together, then put your hands in again and draw the dough together into a ball.

4 Pick off small pieces of dough and roll them into balls, each about the size of a cherry. Press 8 balls of the cookie dough together into a circle, then repeat to make a further 5 garlands. Place small pieces of glacé cherry or angelica between the balls.

5 Place the cookies in a preheated oven, 190°C (375°F), Gas Mark 5, and bake for about 15 minutes or until pale golden. Just before the end of the cooking time, brush with the remainder of the egg and sprinkle with caster sugar, then return to the oven to finish cooking.

6 Remove the cookies from the oven and allow to cool a little then transfer to a wire rack.

Chunky monkey cookies

Makes 18
Preparation time 15 minutes
Cooking time 8–12 minutes

Packed with colour, these spectacular cookies are always a hit. They will taste just as good if you use dark chocolate and apricots instead of white chocolate and cherries.

125 g (4 oz) butter, plus
   extra for greasing
200 g (7 oz) plain flour
1 teaspoon bicarbonate of
   soda
125 g (4 oz) caster sugar
1 egg
1 tablespoon milk
150 g (5 oz) white chocolate
75 g (3 oz) glacé cherries

1 Grease 2 or 3 baking sheets.

2 Put the flour, bicarbonate of soda and sugar into a large mixing bowl and mix together. Cut the butter into small pieces and add to the bowl. Rub in the butter with your fingertips or an electric mixer until the mixture looks like fine crumbs.

3 Beat together the egg and milk in a cup or mug. Chop the chocolate and cherries into rough pieces on a chopping board, then add all 4 ingredients to the bowl and mix together.

4 Drop heaped dessertspoonfuls of cookie mixture, well spaced apart, on to the baking sheets. Place in a preheated oven, 180°C (350°F), Gas Mark 4, and bake in the oven for 8–12 minutes until lightly browned. Leave the cookies for 2 minutes to harden, then transfer with a palette knife to a wire rack.

Sweetheart cookies

Makes 15
Preparation time 25 minutes
Cooking time 10–12 minutes

A beautiful version of an old children's favourite, the jammy dodger. Not only do these look better, but they taste much better than the shop-bought version.

a little cooking oil, for
  greasing
200 g (7 oz) plain flour, plus
  extra for dusting
25 g (1 oz) custard powder
50 g (2 oz) caster sugar
150 g (5 oz) butter, at room
  temperature
1 egg yolk
4 tablespoons seedless
  raspberry jam
sifted icing sugar, to
  decorate

1 Lightly brush 2 baking sheets with a little oil.

2 Put the flour, custard powder and sugar into a large mixing bowl. Cut the butter into pieces, then add to the bowl. Rub the butter into the flour mixture between your fingertips to make tiny crumbs.

3 Stir in the egg yolk and mix to a smooth dough, first with a round-bladed knife then with your hands when the dough becomes too stiff to stir.

4 Knead the dough on a lightly floured work surface, then cut it in half and roll out one half until about 5 mm (¼ inch) thick. Stamp out large circles using a 6 cm (2½ inch) fluted round cookie cutter. Cut out little hearts from the centre of half the circles, using a 3 cm (1¼ inch) heart-shaped cookie cutter, and lift out with the end of a small sharp knife. Transfer the rounds to the oiled baking sheets. Squeeze the trimmings together and roll out with the remaining dough, stamping out shapes until you have 15 circles with heart-shaped centres cut out and 15 whole circles.

5 Place the cookies in a preheated oven, 160°C (325°F), Gas Mark 3, and bake for 10–12 minutes (slightly less for the heart-stamped ones) until they are pale golden. Loosen the cookies with a palette knife and leave to cool on the baking sheets. They can be stored in an airtight tin for up to 2 days.

6 To serve, spread the jam over the whole cookies, top with the heart-stamped ones, then dust with a little sifted icing sugar.

Sesame and maple syrup flapjacks

Makes 9
Preparation time 15 minutes
Cooking time 20–25 minutes

If your children like flapjacks, they will love these yummy oat biscuits. A perfect addition to any lunchbox, these will give your kids a real energy boost.

200 g (7 oz) butter
200 g (7 oz) soft light brown sugar
5 tablespoons maple syrup or golden syrup
50 g (2 oz) sesame seeds, plus 1 extra tablespoon for sprinkling
250 g (8 oz) oats

1 Line a 20 cm (8 inch) square shallow cake tin with nonstick baking paper by cutting a square of paper a little larger than the tin, then snip into the corners and press the paper into the tin.

2 Put the butter, sugar and syrup in a medium saucepan and heat gently, stirring from time to time with a wooden spoon, until completely melted.

3 Take the saucepan off the heat and stir in the sesame seeds and oats. Spoon the mixture into the lined tin and press flat with the back of a metal spoon. Sprinkle with the extra 1 tablespoon of sesame seeds.

4 Place the flapjack in a preheated oven, 180°C (350°F), Gas Mark 4, and bake for 20–25 minutes until it is golden brown and just beginning to darken around the edges of the tin. Leave to cool for 10 minutes. Mark the flapjack into squares with a round-bladed knife and leave to harden and cool completely.

5 Lift the paper and flapjack out of the tin, peel off the paper and put the flapjack on a chopping board. Cut into 9 pieces to serve. The flapjacks can be stored in an airtight tin for up to 3 days.

Millionaire's shortbread

Makes 18
Preparation time 20 minutes, plus chilling
Cooking time 30–35 minutes

a little cooking oil, for greasing
250 g (8 oz) plain flour
25 g (1 oz) cornflour
50 g (2 oz) caster sugar
175 g (6 oz) butter, at room temperature

For the topping
2 tablespoons golden syrup
75 g (3 oz) butter
75 g (3 oz) light muscovado sugar
3 tablespoons double cream
75 g (3 oz) dark or milk chocolate
75 g (3 oz) white chocolate (optional)

A very decadent treat, this is always a winner! Kids and adults alike will adore the crunchy shortbread base, yummy caramel filling and squiggly chocolate topping.

1   Lightly brush a small roasting tin with a little oil.

2   Put the flour, cornflour and sugar in a large mixing bowl. Cut the butter into pieces, then add to the bowl. Rub the butter into the flour mixture between your fingertips to make tiny crumbs. Squeeze the crumbs together, then tip the mixture into the oiled tin and press flat with your hands.

3   Place the shortbread in a preheated oven, 180°C (350°F), Gas Mark 4, and bake for 20–25 minutes until it is pale golden.

4   When the shortbread is almost ready, put the golden syrup, butter and sugar in a small saucepan and heat until the butter has melted. Boil for 1 minute. Stir in the cream and cook for 30 seconds. Pour the hot toffee over the hot shortbread, smooth flat then leave to cool and set.

5   To finish, break the dark or milk chocolate into pieces and put them in another bowl. Place the bowl over a saucepan of just boiled water and leave for 4–5 minutes until melted. Drizzle spoonfuls of the melted chocolate in wiggly scribble-like lines over the set toffee. Chill for 15 minutes. Melt the white chocolate, if using, in the same way as the dark, then drizzle it over the top. Chill until set. To serve, cut the shortbread into 18 pieces and lift them out of the tin.

Scottish shortbread

Makes 8
Preparation time 15 minutes
Cooking time 20–25 minutes

Simple to make, shortbread is not only a superb tea-time snack, but goes well with stewed fruit or yogurt to make a truly scrumptious pudding.

175 g (6 oz) plain flour
125 g (4 oz) butter, at room temperature
50 g (2 oz) caster sugar, plus a little extra for sprinkling

1 Put the flour in a mixing bowl. Cut the butter into pieces, then add to the flour along with the sugar.

2 Rub the butter into the flour mixture between your fingertips to make tiny crumbs, or use an electric mixer. Squeeze the crumbs together with your hands until they stick together.

3 Tip the mixture into a 20 cm (8 inch) fluted-edged, loose-bottomed flan tin (there is no need to grease it first) and press flat using your hands. If you don't have a flan tin, press the shortbread into a round on a baking sheet. Decorate all around the edge of the shortbread by pressing your finger into the edge. Prick the middle with a fork and sprinkle with a little extra sugar.

4 Place the shortbread in a preheated oven, 160°C (325°F), Gas Mark 3, and bake for 20–25 minutes until it is pale golden. Take the shortbread out of the oven and mark it into 8 triangular-shaped pieces. Leave the shortbread to cool in the tin, then cut the shortbread pieces right through and lift them out of the tin. They can be stored in an airtight tin for up to 5 days.

Index

Acknowledgements

Octopus Publishing Group Limited/Vanessa Davies 1, 2, 4, 6, 7, 8, 9, 10, 11, 12, 14, 17, 19, 20, 23, 24, 27, 28, 31, 37, 64, 76, 78, 80, 83, 85, 86, 90, 93, 94, 97, 98, 101, 104, 107, 111, 112, 115, 119, 120, 123, 124; /David Jordan 45, 49, 52, 56, 63, 70, 74; /Lis Parsons 32, 35, 38, 41, 51, 55, 59, 67, 73, 103; /Peter Pugh-Cook 42, 46, 60, 69, 89, 108, 116.

Executive Editor: Nicola Hill
Managing Editor: Clare Churly
Deputy Creative Director: Karen Sawyer
Designer: Janis Utton
Senior Production Controller: Martin Croshaw